The Fast Learner's Guide

HOW TO LEARN ANY SKILLS OR SUBJECTS QUICK
AND DRAMATICALLY IMPROVE YOUR SHORT-TERM
MEMORY IN A SHORT TIME

BRUCE WALKER

Contents

Introduction

Think back to your high school days. What type of student – or more appropriately "learner" – were you. Did you have to drag every book home and study just to pass the courses?

Or were you the type of learner that could read the material once (or so it seemed to everyone else) and have the information digested?

It's an age-old question for students and now with the growing mountain of information in the world, it's a question we all ask ourselves: Why do some people learn faster than others?

Let's get to the next question that everyone is really thinking: How can I learn faster?

This question is more valid and more crucial than ever. The amount of knowledge that has been created in some shape has been increasing since the beginning of the twenty century. The legendary Buckminster Fuller noticed this phenomenon and dubbed it the "Knowledge Doubling Curve."

He noted that up until the twentieth-century knowledge doubled at a rate of approximately every 100 years. After World War II, knowledge doubled at a speed of about every quarter of a century.

Today, knowledge is still accumulating rapidly, but depending on the type of knowledge and who's quoting the statistics, you'll receive a few different rates. Take the growing field of nanotechnology, for example. The knowledge in this field is doubling every two years as we discover more about its exact operations. Clinical knowledge, for example, doubles at a rate of every year and a half. A mere eighteen months.

It's generally accepted that on average, the amount of human knowledge doubles once every thirteen months. That's perilously close to once a year.

These statistics are enough to make your mind reel. Even if you attempt to keep this rate growth within your field of expertise, you'd still discover how much more knowledge there is in the world than there was even a mere year before.

The bottom line is that as the years progress, you may be expected in your job or in your college classroom, to learn more facts, statistics and concepts than any generation up to now.

That's no small feat. You can see now why the question "How can I learn faster?" is even more imperative than ever before.

But you're right to ask the first question as well, why do some individuals learn faster than others? If science could unlock that mystery, then perhaps it could help us put that information to use in your schooling, your career, or just your daily life.

The Answers Are Already Here

It's not surprising to learn then that the questions are already being answered even as you read this, thanks to some stunning new research. It's complicated, admittedly, but the results seem to be clear and quite easy to understand.

Let's start with a variation of that question, one everyone who's ever ventured into new terrain with a project has probably asked himself. Why do some people learn from their mistakes faster than others?

According to Jason Moser, of Michigan State University, the brain reacts quickly when you make a mistake. Actually, it reacts in two distinct, nearly instantaneous ways. The first action your brain takes is referred to as "error-related negativity." It occurs 50 milliseconds after you make a mistake. This reaction takes place in the portion of the brain that deals with the monitoring of your behavior, anticipation of rewards, and regulating attention.

We've all experienced this reaction, even if we didn't know why. Seconds after you do something, you realize it was wrong. That's your "error-related negativity" setting in. Good to know, isn't it?

But nearly as fast, there's another reaction your brain experiences, this one about 500 to 1,000 milliseconds after your action. This one is called "error positivity," and is closely related to your awareness. This reaction takes place when you pay attention to the mistake and think about its disappointing results.

The results of Moser's experiments strongly suggest two very important results for the purposes of learning faster. The first is that those individuals with the larger "error-related negativity" response coupled with the larger "error positivity" response are those who learn at a quicker pace than others.

It seems their brains immediately start to formulate a Plan B, as it were, which inherently means, it's figuring out how you can learn from this mistake.

If this is the case, you may say, how can I ever hope to learn faster. From all the information it seems as if you're doomed to one learning speed. Not so. These reactions are actually shaped by your current beliefs about learning.

Fixed and Learned Mindsets

There are two ways people look at their ability to learn. These perceptions are called mindsets. The first is that individuals tend to have a "fixed" conception of their ability to learn. These individuals believe that they only have a certain amount of intelligence and resign themselves into thinking that are areas they'll never be able to understand because of this.

In the second perspective, certain individuals take what is called the "growth mindset" and it holds that the mind is capable of learning beyond your stated "intelligence level" given the proper conditions and conditioning.

In other words, the fixed mindset chalks mistake up to your inherent lack of talent or intelligence. The growth mindset sees mistakes and failures as an "essential precursor" to gaining more knowledge.

Now, let's get back to the initial question: Why do some individuals learn quicker than others? The bottom line is because they don't dwell on their mistakes very long or doubt that they can eventually learn from them. This means while their error mindset kicks in, the "error positivity" portion of the brain starts responding quickly.

Let's take a look at two high school students in order to make this concept a bit more practical. Both students have about the same amount of talent and intelligence. Both bombed miserably on a history test. The one student chalks it up to not being good in history. "I'll never be able to learn this stuff," he sighs.

The second student, however, comes from a mind-growth consciousness and knows that he can ace the next test simply by learning from the mistakes he made not only on the test but perhaps even in his method of studying for it.

The next test comes around. Sure enough, the student with the fixed mindset again performs poorly. The student who was determined to learn from the first experience has received an amazingly high score.

Which student are you? If you believe you're the one who can't learn or can't learn fast enough, then this book is for you. You can change yourself from a person who dwells on the mistakes of the past and transforms yourself into the one who devises ways in which to learn faster.

In this book, you'll be exposed to all sorts of methods to help you learn faster, remember what you learn longer and change your limiting beliefs about your abilities and intelligence.

You'll discover this book covers everything from styles of learning (visual, auditory and kinesthetic) to how taking care of your body can actually improve your mind. We'll talk about the importance of deconstruction in learning as well as the power of the eighty-twenty rule.

Think your memory is static? Think again. A good memory is essential for any quick learner and this book will teach you tips, tricks, and techniques to improve yours. This book will also show you why certain distractions interfere with your ability to learn.

Are you ready to discover how quickly you can learn? Let's get to the first chapter, it's all about positioning yourself in the best physical shape.

Tick. Tick. Tick. Do you hear that? That's a clock ticking off the amount of growing knowledge out there waiting for you to learn all about it.

CHAPTER 1:

⁓

Putting yourself in the Best Position

Before you can learn at your optimal level your body has to be sound. Science has not only finally discovered the mind-body connection but is learning bit by bit how it works. What are the three most important components to create the best mind-body connection?

Sleep, a healthy diet, and physical exercise. If you're serious about learning faster, then you'll want to improve all three of these areas of your life. The following information not only explains why this connection exists, but it also helps you take full advantage of it.

Learning and Sleep

The impact of sleep on your memory and your ability to learn is a vivid example of how scientists are recognizing that connection. Sleep, scientists now know, is vital to the learning process. Think back to your college days when you believed that all you needed to do was "pull that all-nighter" in order to ace your exam. An all-nighter is an act of staying up all night studying in hopes of cramming what you should have been learning all term into your brain in a short period of time.

While the entire picture hasn't been uncovered yet, it seems quite obvious, after extensive research on the subject, that our brain is consolidating and "filing away" the learning we accumulated for that day.

It seems obvious then, that if you want to learn faster, you should pay more attention to your sleep patterns.

How Sleep Improves Learning

The latest research indicates that an adequate amount of sleep, typically defined as seven and a half hours, helps expedite learning through two means. First, it enables you to focus better. According to the Harvard Medical Center blog, a person who isn't receiving enough sleep finds it difficult to focus. It's clear, without proper focus, efficient learning will never occur.

But even beyond that, getting the recommended number of hours of sleep helps to consolidate your memory, which is absolutely necessary if you want to learn and retain your new-found knowledge.

Exactly how your body does this, though, still isn't well understood. Scientists do know this. It seems to be a three-step process. The first step is the acquisition process. This is the portion in which you introduce new information or knowledge to your brain. This is your brain reading and studying.

The second step is in the consolidation of this material. It's the way your brain ensures that what you've introduced it becomes firmly embedded into your mind. The third step is the recall portion of learning. That, naturally, is the process of retrieving this information when it's needed.

How many hours of sleep is optimum for learning?

The number of hours of sleep needed for the quickest learning varies from person to person. Some individuals thrive on four or five hours. Thomas A. Edison was reputed to be one of these.

You'll have to find your own sleep patterns and the amount of sleep at which you feel your best. Usually, seven and a half hours are recommended. How do you know if you're receiving enough sleep? There are certain telltale signs. For example, if you need to drink more than one cup of coffee in a day to keep your body and mind going, chances are good you're not getting enough sleep during the night.

If you have trouble sleeping at night here are a few tips to help you fall asleep faster and sleep better.

1. Increase your level of magnesium.

Without a doubt, magnesium is probably the most potent of the trace minerals for inducing sleep. It not only helps to regulate your hormonal balance, but magnesium also can improve your brain function. It seems increasing magnesium is a win-win situation.

A recent study revealed that more than half of Americans – 68 percent to be exact – are not receiving enough of this mineral. What's more startling is that approximately 20 percent of those individuals aren't even receiving half of the recommended daily amount.

Adults need approximately 420 mg of this trace mineral a day.

2. Raise your blood pressure slightly.

This is a tricky recommendation. Many individuals decide to perform a full-scale workout right before bedtime. That will increase your blood pressure too much and you'll find yourself tossing and turning all night.

You'd be far better off to do some light yoga postures or go out for a leisurely walk before bedtime. That should raise your blood pressure just enough to help you sleep like a baby.

3. Avoid eating sugar-laden foods.

These foods will only act as a catalyst to keep you awake. Think about how toddlers act when they eat too much sugar. Your adult body acts in the same manner. You probably don't always make that connection.

4. Don't drink or eat anything with caffeine before bedtime.

Consider this, it takes approximately six hours for your body to cleanse the caffeine from only half a cup of coffee from your system. Not only can coffee make it more difficult to fall asleep at night, but the caffeine can also wake you more frequently through the night, reducing both the quantity and quality of your sleep.

Eating Healthy

Your brain gets quite a workout when you're learning new material. But did you ever stop to think how much nutrition it gobbles up during this period? If you're not giving your brain the food it needs, you'll never be able to step up your learning curve.

So what's the number one brain food? Some may speculate fish and others may say sweet potatoes, your brain has only one fuel source. That's glucose, also known as sugar. There are several ways to get this source.

Your brain can use glucose directly from many foods you're probably already eating, including grains, legumes, fruits and vegetables, and dairy products. When you eat carbohydrates, the food breaks down and forms sugar in your stomach before it gets absorbed into your bloodstream. Once the glucose reaches your brain, it's then converted into chemical energy that your brain cells can use.

Your brain cells need twice as much energy than the rest of your body. Because your brain can't store the glucose, it depletes all too rapidly during intense mental activity – like learning. Recent research, as a matter of fact, reveals that mental concentration depletes the sugar in the areas of the brain closely associated with the portions that regulate memory and learning.

You may think this new research gives you carte blanche to run out to the store while you're studying and pick up all sorts of candy bars and sugary drinks. Stop. Before you go any further, you need to know that's not how the body works. Instead of taking in your glucose through simple sugars, you need to ingest them through complex carbohydrates. Here are some ideal candidates for foods to eat while you're learning.

- Beans

- Brown Rice

- Lentils

- Oatmeal

- Rye

- Sweet potatoes

Not only should you be eating foods like these, but you also need to keep a steady supply of food to your brain. That's why Dr. Mehmet Oz recommends this simple eating plan – especially when you're busy studying and learning.

It's called "eating in threes." First, you should eat every three hours. Then when you do eat, your meals should contain one-third protein, one-third healthy fats and one-third complex carbohydrates.

Dr. Oz urges you to make good choices when it comes to the foods you consume. Below are just a few of the possibilities in the "eating in threes" strategy. The following are some healthy proteins that will help fuel your brain: Cheese, chicken, eggs, fish, shellfish, Greek yogurt, and quinoa.

The following fiber foods also make excellent "brain food": Almonds, apples, carrots, barley, cantaloupe, strawberries, watermelon, lentils, oranges, and pears. And finally, and perhaps the most imperative healthy fats that your brain will gobble up: peanut butter, walnuts, pistachios, and avocado.

This is your Brain with Physical Energy

Having just learned the vital role food plays in brain health, it should come as no surprise that physical exercise is a necessary component of speeding up the learning process.

Physical exercise, in fact, increases your learning speed in several ways. First, exercise, especially cardiovascular exercise, increases your heart rate. That, in turn, pumps more oxygen to your brain. But more than that, exercise also releases a myriad of hormones, all necessary to nourish the growth of your brain cells.

If those two reasons weren't enough, there's a third reason that regular exercise is required to keep your brain in tip-top learning shape. Physical activity actually stimulates the plasticity of the brain by stimulating the growth of new connections not only among cells but in a wide swath of important cortical areas of the brain. In plain English, this means the physical activity makes it easier for the brain to grow new connections.

Who knew that the "runner's high" that many who exercise experience can also help in the learning process and improve your memory? According to a recent Swedish scientific study, the "runner's high" is associated with increased cell growth in the hippocampus. That's the same area of the brain that's charged with learning and memory.

Putting an exercise plan into action

From the results of the research, you've already recognized, I'm sure, that any exercise that aids your heart will also help your brain learn faster. That means you're probably thinking that aerobic exercise is a good choice. And you're right. Aerobic exercise improves the way your brain works and at the same time acts as what some scientists refer to as a "first-aid kit" for damaged brain cells.

The best time to exercise, by the way, is in the morning even before you go to work. A morning workout "spikes" your brain activity, preparing you for the mental stresses for what lies ahead in your day. But more than that, the physical activity aids in increasing your retaining new information.

CHAPTER 2:

⁓

Knowing your Learning Style

How do you learn?

If you're like most people you haven't given it much thought. You also probably assumed you didn't have much of a choice when it came to choose learning styles.

The bottom line is you probably didn't even know there were "learning styles" from which you can choose. There are three major learning styles according to recent research. The problem is you may not always be able to choose the one most suited to you all the time. However, knowing which one suits you, will help you customize your own personal learning agenda to enable to achieve your goals as rapidly as possible.

It appears, according to educational specialists, that everyone favors one of three learning styles. When you discover your specific style, you'll see significant gains in the amount of information you retain and the speed with which you attain it. You may even learn best through a combination of two or all of them.

The three styles are:

- Visual

- Auditory

- Kinesthetic

Visually dominant learners reach their goals faster and retain more of what they learn from information retrieved through studying diagrams, charts, and pictures. In addition, you can tell if you learn more through visual means, listen to yourself talk when you're studying, or learn something new. Visual learners tend to use expressions like the following:

I get the picture, now.

I see what you mean.

What's your view on this?

Perhaps you learn quicker when you listen to the material. You'd be an auditory learner, then. You may prefer to learn through podcasts or even audiobooks. In this case, you respond best to lectures or group discussions. If this is the case, then you'll also learn more rapidly if you hear your own voice. One of the methods you can use is to repeat back what someone tells you. You could also paraphrase out loud information you read. In this way, it'll stick with you longer.

If your brain does respond best to the auditory method, you'll find yourself commenting on your learning process using phrases similar to these:

That sounds good to me.

I hear what you're saying.

That rings a bell.

If you learn through the kinesthetic method, you learn quicker and retain more knowledge when you participate in physical activities and "hands-on" assignments. The best way to describe this method is that you learn while doing. Perhaps you think there's nothing better than on-the-job training.

You'll also know if you're a person who prefers active learning when you hear yourself talk in these terms as you digest information:

How does that grab you?

That feels right to me.

Let me try it.

There's also a fourth method of learning sometimes included in this group and that's the reading and writing style. You'll know immediately if you learn through this method. Think back first to your grade school days. What was the quickest method you used to help you learn your spelling words? Did you write each word out five or more times the night before a test?

When you were in college or high school, did you take your notes out the night before an exam and pare them down by writing an even shorter list of notes? You may learn best through the reading and writing methods if you reread your textbook prior to your exams.

When you can decide on your learning style or styles then you can continue your studies with greater confidence. Knowing how you learn best is also a great platform to help you implement another technique of accelerated learning. That's immersion.

The Role of Immersion in the Learning Process

This learning process has been called an "educational powerhouse."

What is it? Immersion. If you've ever studied a foreign language, then you may be familiar with the concept. In the case of accelerated learning, it uses the same idea as immersing yourself in a foreign language only the subject matter is different.

If you're already working in your chosen career, congratulations. You have the best perspective on which to use this process. It's called on-the-job training. For all intents and purposes, it's a form of immersion because it engages all three learning styles.

Without a doubt, you find that you're learning more quickly than reading that same information from a book. Not only that, learning the same material from a book doesn't even begin to give you a flavor of what's it's like to really be in that job or situation.

What's occurring during a good session of immersion or on-the-job training is nothing less than an increase in the rate of growth of specific brain-body connections – the basic building blocks of all learning. Recent scientific studies are proving that the art of learning – regardless of subject matter – is an effort that involves both the body and the mind working in tandem.

The concept of immersion is nearly the ideal method of learning. Why? Because in addition to being exposed to all the figures, facts and statistics, you're also absorbing the dynamics of the relationship among team members and how that alone can make or break any business project or process.

There's still another reason why immersion is such an effective learning tool. It increases your contact with and use of the material. On-the-job training also increases a person's motivation to learn.

In effect, learning becomes a personal effort, driven by personal desires to be attained and dreams to be fulfilled as well as the professional goals set before you. If you're already working in your career and would like to learn more to attain that promotion or enlarge your relationships, you're already perfectly placed.

If you're a student eager to learn faster, consider obtaining an internship in the career of your choice. Participating in a summer internship program, for example, can be the perfect motivator to return to school with a renewed sense of learning. Once you experience the traits and talents you need for the job, you appreciate why you need to learn certain subjects. When other students are grumbling about learning algebra, for example, you'll already know why it's important for the position you have in mind – and just get down to learning it.

Taking Notes

So let's say you've already immersed yourself in your on-the-job training and are back at school, highly motivated to learn. But you find yourself in a quandary. You don't seem to be an effective "note taker." Try as you might capture the essence of your professors' lessons, it somehow eludes you.

How are you recording your notes? No, it' a pertinent question. Today many students take their laptop computers into class and key in the notes onto a word document as the professor is speaking.

Others prefer it the old-fashioned way, taking notes by hand and then perhaps transferring them to a computer later. You may be anticipating the next line in this chapter to read. Either way, you take your notes is effective.

But that's not the case at all. A new scientific study recently revealed that those who took notes by hand had a higher retention rate than those who used a laptop. The scientists segregated students into two groups, and they all watched the same TED talk. At the end of the talk, they were given some tasks to perform, designed to distract them from thinking about the talk they had recently heard.

After about thirty minutes, both groups were asked a series of questions on the talk. These questions covered both the major facts of the talk as well as some conceptual questions.. While both groups – those who took notes with their computers and those who took notes by hand – performed equally well on factual material, there was a difference in performance regarding conceptual questions. Those individuals instructed to take handwritten notes significantly performed better than those who keyed the notes into their laptops.

Not only that, but the students who took handwritten notes still possessed better recall a week after the talks, scientists said. The scientists believe the difference involves the way in which individuals process the information when they first hear it. When they're strictly using the laptop, the individuals appear to concentrate their efforts on capturing the speaker's words nearly word for word.

When they take pen to paper there's more paraphrasing occurring, of necessity. Perhaps this, the scientist speculates, force the students to not only reword it but conceptualize the material at the same time.

The bottom line seems to be that taking notes the old-fashioned way with pen and paper is still the best method.

The more you know about your mind and body work together to help you learn as quickly the easier the process will be. In the next chapter, you'll learn about the very simple idea of "deconstruction" in order to avoid being intimated by a mound of information that appears impossible to penetrate.

CHAPTER 3:

~

The "Deconstruction" of Learning

While you're preparing your body for a good "mental workout" by physically getting into shape, you probably have had some time to think about how you're going to approach your new learning journey.

Or perhaps not. Many individuals don't give the concept of learning new subjects or more about familiar topics much thought. They go to the library, find several books about the subject and then they believe that they can digest the information in these volumes.

Sometimes they can. But that's not the fastest way to learn something – history, quantum physics, even knitting. And remember, what you want to do is become a quick learner.

So the next time you're tempted to run to the library or surf the net for all the information you can find, stop yourself. First, learning in this fashion is intimidating. It's difficult enough to understand physics for the average person. But to dig right into it and hope you'll come out with some insights . . . well, good luck with that.

Here's a technique that all individuals who learn quickly do, whether they're aware of it or not. It's called deconstruction and it works much like the word. Instead of jumping into the middle of the fray, as it were, picking up a bit of information here, a little knowledge there about a subject, sit back and examine the whole of what they want to learn. Then sit back and break the topic down into manageable, bite-size pieces.

In this way, the task of learning doesn't appear quite so daunting. Secondly, you're learning from the ground floor up. You can't learn calculus, for example, if you can't multiply. If you think about how you learned as you went through your different grade levels in school, it makes perfect sense.

Here's the idea of deconstruction the way my friend, the freelance writer, uses it. This may be an extreme version of it, but it works for her. She gets many assignments to write non-fiction books. Sometimes she's familiar with a topic, sometimes she's not.

When she gets assigned a topic, she knows next to nothing about she moves immediately to two locations. The children's department at the local library and every children's education website that talks about the subject.

She breaks down the information to the easiest she can understand. She figures if it's written for a child, she should be able to grasp the fundamentals and then build upon that. It doesn't take long, of course, to master the children's books on any given topic, but in that short amount of time, she at least has an idea of what she needs to know next.

Now, that doesn't mean that every time you need to learn something you have to run to children's books. It's just a vivid and simple illustration of how deconstruction can work.

There are several steps to deconstruction to keep in mind. If you follow these broad principles, just once, you'll discover how simple and quick learning can be:

1. Get to the basics of the material right away.

Do this even if you think you have a good grasp of the subject matter. If nothing else it makes a great review for yourself. The basics are the fundamentals of the topic that needs to be kept constantly in mind.

2. Discover the principles of this topic.

These are the "rules" of the topic that never change, regardless of what else may about this material. For example, one of the principles of basic addition you were taught, no doubt, was the "communitive" law. If you don't remember the name, that's quite understandable. Basically, it states that the order of the items you're adding doesn't matter. Your total will always be the same. For example, if two plus three equals five, then three plus two also equals five. Always. Never fails.

Other subjects have principles like this. How can you use this to your advantage when you're learning? If you discover a piece of information that violates this principle, then you can immediately discard it. Don't build upon it.

You'll know immediately it's wrong and won't have to waste your time testing it.

3. Build your other knowledge of this topic on those two ideas.

If you do that then you'll have a solid foundation and you'll be surprised at how quickly your learning will be facilitated.

Now that you know the basics of deconstructing your topic, you're ready for a few pointers on how to use this quickly and to your best advantage.

1. Get motivated.

Without motivation, nothing gets down. What motivation do you have to learn this topic? Is it an intrinsic desire that you've possessed all your life or is it just a passing "I wish I could do this?" type desire.

The more motivated you are to learn a new subject, the quicker you will. Many individuals think they want to learn a new language. But without a burning desire or need to, they may never learn it.

Do you need to learn this subject in order to graduate from college? Then the guess is you're highly motivated. But if you're learning Spanish just on a whim, you may find it more difficult to learn.

2. Set goals.

Here is where many people, regardless of their motivation, trip up. They set their goals, but they aren't realistic ones. When they fail to meet them, they blame themselves for not being smart enough. In effect, they've set themselves up for failure and they fall back into that "fixed" mindset of learning. "See I told you I wasn't smart enough to learn this," they rationalize.

3. Celebrate when you reach a goal

That's right! When you achieve your first goal, celebrate and reward yourself in some way. You decide the appropriate celebration. My friend, the writer, rewarded herself when she reached her goal of having her first novel published with a small celebration of her closest friends at a local café and one (only one) glass of the finest scotch the establishment stocked.

But you don't have to wait so long in a project. However, you decide to break your learning goals down, make sure you take time to reward yourself when you've accomplished it. This will assure that you'll be ready to tackle the next goal.

4. Create a schedule.

Here's another way to implement your deconstruction technique. When you set a goal, set a schedule for it to be completed at the same time. Again, this can be a tricky act.

If you set yourself too tight a schedule and you're not able to keep it you may feel like a failure.

5. Be flexible

This brings us to your next necessity when breaking down your topic for learning. Flexibility. You may not always meet your schedule. If you can't meet it, that doesn't mean the zombie apocalypse is upon you. It just means you have to adjust your timing a bit.

Waste as little time as possible brooding over the missed date (or to use the terms we used in the intro- duction, don't dwell on the "error-related negativity"), instead, get the "error positivity" portion of your brain working on the problem and set another time slot for reaching that goal. If you must adjust the rest of your schedule, do so then. After that, forget about it and forge on.

5. Record and Review your Progress

At the very least, this reminds you of how far you've come. By doing this, it provides you with the self-con- fidence you need to move on to the next step of your learning phase. It also raises your self-esteem.

In other words, it'll help to nudge your innate be- lief system from one of a fixed learning mindset ("I can't possibly learn this!) to one of a growth mentality ("Wow! When I apply myself to this stuff, I really can learn it!).

Once this occurs, then they'll be no stopping or slowing you down. In the next chapter, you'll learn about how the 80/20 rule can help you accelerate your learning even more without sacrificing quality.

CHAPTER 4:

~

The Power of the 80/20 Rule

I spent a lot of time studying that entire section, yet there wasn't one question on the exam from it.

How many times have you complained about this? You study thoroughly. You're disgruntled after the test because you believe you "wasted" your time by loading your mind with facts and figures you didn't use.

Why does that occur? And even a more important question: How can you decrease the risk of it happening in the future?

The problem began by giving equal weight to all the material. As with any body of information, some of it will be more important than others. The good news is that you can prevent this from happening again by employing the Pareto Rule?

Never heard of it? You might know it by its more common name: the 80/20 rule. It's a phenomenon that states that 20 percent of your efforts yield 80 percent of your results. While many individuals apply it to their business in which 20 percent of their customers provide them with 80 of theirs.

Italian economist Vilfredo Pareto identified this trend at the beginning of the twentieth century. It was, however, expanded in the 1940s by Joseph Juran saw its applicability to every area of business.

And learning.

In fact, if you keep the 80/20 rule in mind as you study you may be able to save yourself valuable time, especially since your goal is to learn more in the least amount of time.

So how do you apply it to accelerated learning? You need to keep in mind that 20 percent of your efforts yield 80 percent of your new-found knowledge. Before you think that the implication is that you can skate through this learning process without working at it, that's not what the rule means.

The law of 80/20 will give you the confidence to discern which information may be valuable and which isn't. In the past, you may have studied by giving equal weight – and equal study time – to all areas of the text or your notes. This usually isn't the case when you get to the test, though.

If you've ever learned English as a second language, think back to how it was taught. If it were conversational English, you learned words and phrases dealing with ordinary everyday conversations. You began and most of your efforts were concentrated on the most common words you would use in a conversation if you've just met a person.

You wouldn't learn English words that were irrelevant to your purpose. This idea can be applied to any topic and to any learning situation – whether you're in business or in an academic setting.

It doesn't mean that the other areas of the English language aren't important because they certainly are. It does mean is that you now can allow many of those rules and that vocabulary to sink into your brain at a slower more natural rate.

You can utilize the 80/20 rule in at least two ways if you're serious about your accelerated learning program. First, let's explore what this means for your use of time. If 20 percent of your efforts yield 80 percent of your knowledge, then you need to evaluate exactly how you spend that 20 percent of your time.

The point is that not all of our efforts are equally relevant. The vast majority of us have been taught that if you're not working hard – eight hours a day, 40 hours a week – then you couldn't possibly get ahead. Or in your case, you couldn't possibly learn at the rate you need to learn given all the information bombarding us every day.

All you need to do is to be a bit more discerning in how you use your time. Think of the Mad Hatter in *Alice in Wonderland* dashing around singing, "I'm late! I'm late! For a very important date!" The truth of the matter is that some "dates" are more important than others. Your goal is to decide what in your learning schedule is vital and what isn't. Then you focus on what you believe are the most salient points of the material.

The chances then of you studying the "wrong" information that doesn't form the bulk of the body of knowledge you need to know is greatly reduced. Sure, you may miss a question because it popped up on a test and you decided other aspects of the information were more important. Chances are then that the bulk of what you got right on the test far outweighs this one incorrect answer.

The truth of the matter is when you're out to learn more and faster as in accelerated learning, you can get caught up in jumping around among all sorts of materials, trying to learn what you can here, there and everywhere. According to the Pareto Rule, it seems this type of unrestrained and disorganized attempt at studying will only waste your time.

It makes much more sense to focus on the two or three most important themes in a topic. Learn these like the back of your hand. Once you do this, you'll immediately know where you need to go from there.

Deconstruction Learning and the Pareto Rule

Using the deconstruction method associated with accelerated learning is a great way to put the Pareto Rule into use. As you analyze what parts of the subject matter are crucial and learn them immediately, you'll automatically find yourself spending 20 percent of your time on these items, which in turn will provide you with about 80 percent of your results.

The idea isn't to indiscriminately slash the time you spend learning a topic. The idea is to analyze the body of information and then make some well-informed choices. When you first start this process, you make a misjudgment or two,

Don't allow that to discourage you or worse yet to deter you from implementing this principle. The more you use deconstruction, the better your decision-making process will be and the more accurate, the more effective and precise.

Now that you're well-armed with a variety of learning techniques, you're ready to dig in and get busy – almost! In the final chapters, you'll learn some of the best-kept secrets (and some that are more widely known) to developing a better memory and creating a space for learning.

CHAPTER 5:

~

Secrets to Having a Good Memory

For most of us, however, your body creates and retains memories that at times elude you. If you're like most of us, you marvel at what you've learned and retained from your fourth-grade teacher. On the flip side, try as you might, you can't recall much, if anything, of what you learned in your college American history course. All you can do is stand back for a moment and ask why.

The why of a good memory is obviously beyond the scope of this book. But, regardless of that, there are a few practical ways you can improve your memory. Think of your memory as your brain's notepad. Your working memory, in effect, is only a temporary storage room for new information.

Let's say you've just been introduced to someone. You retain this information only if it's relevant to you. Once you've determined that you no longer need her name, your memory will disregard it. If the person remains in your life and her name stays relevant to you safely tucked into your long-term memory.

You can see then that short-term memory is essential to you on a daily basis. You can also understand that your life would be much easier if you could strengthen your memory base. Up to this point, you may have thought you have been stuck with the memory you have at the moment.

That's, oh, so not true. There are numbers of ways you can improve and strengthen your memory with even just a bit of effort. Think of the implications this potentially "new, improved" memory could make your efforts in your accelerated learning program.

Some of the tips and secrets presented here may seem obvious, but if you're not doing even these obvious activities, your memory won't improve. Once you find a secret or two you think you can include in your life, then begin to perform them immediately. Make it a part of your daily habits and you'll be strengthening your memory painlessly and nearly effortlessly.

Memory Strengthening Secret #1: Meditation

Disappointed? You may have thought that the first secret would be something a bit more exotic. While daily meditation may not be exciting, the latest research has shown it to be a highly effective technique to give your memory that boost.

But that's not all. It also has confirmed that you can improve your memory through meditation in as little as eight days. That's right! In a bit more than a week, you can concentrate better which can potentially help to accelerate your learning.

Not only that but if you stick with the power of meditation, you'll find that after two weeks, your scores on standardized tests may also improve.

Meditation as a memory strengthener is certainly a counterintuitive result. Who thought, after all, that something like meditation, whose goal is to empty your mind, how can it strengthen your memory? The entire process is not thoroughly known. What little is known is that while you meditate, your brain stops processing information at the same activity level as it does during the day. Part of the answer comes from which brain waves are in use during the still, quiet moments of meditation.

When you're in meditation, beta brain waves which have been busy processing information while you've been studying, abruptly drop. This signals to your brain it's time for the second phase of learning and that's memory consolidation. Therefore, if you meditate throughout the day, you're giving your mind time to classify and consolidate this new information, not unlike what happens when you sleep on your newfound learning.

Memory Strengthening Secret #2: Caffeine

Scientists have performed quite a bit of research about caffeine intake prior to studying and memory performance. For those of you who love coffee are probably a bit disappointed to learn that it doesn't have much of an effect on improving your memory when you drink it before you start your studies.

But it's only been recent that scientists have decided to flip these experiments. What happens when an individual drink a cup of coffee *after* a study session? Ah, now you'll begin to see different results. And if you like coffee, you may want to get ready to prepare yourself a cup – or two.

When caffeine is taken following a "learning task," it appears to improve your memory recall for the next twenty-four hours. The study had the participants memorize a set of images. Later their memories were put to the test by viewing the same images, as well as similar images and finally a completely different set of images.

The individuals were asked to pick out the exact pictures they had been initially asked to memorize. This is typical in studies like this and is called pattern separation and is indicative of a "deeper level of memory retention."

This study concentrated on the potential effects caffeine had on memory consolidation. So it's crucial when the caffeine is ingested following the study session.

Memory Strengthening Secret #3: Chewing Gum

Who would have even thought the act of chewing gum could have any effect – either positive or negative – on your memory?

A scientific study recently revealed that if you chewed gum while you're studying, you will have increased your odds of being more accurate in recalling what you've learned. Not only that, but you may also be able to improve your reaction time.

Scientists aren't sure why that would be except that chewing gum may increase the activity in the hippocampus, a region of the brain that involves memory. The second theory of this effect may be due to the increase of oxygen you receive when you chew the gum. The increased intake of oxygen may boost your ability to focus and pay attention. And that goes a long way to improving your memory.

Memory Strengthening Secret #4: Laughter

Yes, laughter.

While it's long been known that laughter is the best medicine, it's far less known that laughter is also one of the best methods to improve your memory. Laughter, in fact, doesn't target just one area of your brain, though, it actually engages several areas in your brain.

In addition to laughter, just listening to jokes and trying to guess their punch lines activate parts of your brain essential to not only learning but creativity as well.

Don't know exactly how to add the element of laughter in your life? Take a look at some of the suggestions for implementing it into your daily life:

1. Laugh at yourself.

2. When you hear laughter, move close to it.

Individuals are usually more than happy to share a good laugh.

3. Keep a toy on your desk

When things become tense, play with it of course. It's bound to at least bring a smile to your face.

Memory Strengthening Secret #5: Provide your Brain a Good Workout

By the time you're an adult, your brain has developed into an amazing organ. By this time, it's developed literally millions of neural paths that are dedicated to the memory process. Not only that, but your brain is now able to solve familiar problems and take on daily tasks without you even thinking about it.

Pretty amazing, isn't it? There's one snag in all this. If you always stick to using the same neural pathways, then your brain isn't receiving the stimulation it needs to keep your memory as sharp as it should be.

Just like any other muscle in your body, if you don't use it, you'll lose it. Therefore, it only goes to reason the more you use your brain, the better your memory will be.

The question becomes what kind of activities will increase your brain muscle strength. If you choose activities that break your normal routine, you'll do just this. These activities work because they challenge you to create and develop new brain paths.

If you're going to choose this route to help boost your memory, these activities should include four key elements:

1. The activity needs to be an unfamiliar one.

It needs to take you out of your comfort zone and puts your brain to the test.

2. The activity needs to be challenging.

Performing this activity needs to demand your full attention and mental effort.

3. Ideally, it should be an activity on which you can build

This type of memory-boosting activity should start you out on the easiest level and then work your way toward more challenging levels of difficulty. Once the activity begins to feel comfortable, it's a sure sign that you need to up your efforts to the next level.

4. It should be rewarding.

When you choose something that rewards you, it only encourages the learning process. You'll continue to perform this activity at ever-increasing levels of difficulty and find you'll be reaping bigger and better benefits.

Memory Strengthening Secret #6: Live by the Eight Second Rule

When you absolutely, positively need to recall something, do nothing but concentrate on it for a minimum of eight seconds. Don't downplay this advice. While eight seconds may appear to be an inconsequential period, you'd be surprised how long it really is.

Why eight seconds? This is the minimum amount of time your brain needs to send a piece of information from your short-term to your long-term memory.

Memory Strengthening Secret #7: Make a Fist

No, wait! You're not making a fist shove it through the wall because you can't remember where you placed your keys, or the year Warren G. Harding was elected president.

Ideally, you'll want to use a stress ball in relation to this memory-recalling activity. Believe it or not, the very act of clenching your hand into a fist can improve your ability to recall what you've learned. If you're a right-handed ball up your left hand in a fist prior to memorizing a piece of information.

When the time comes to recall this information, you'll clench your left hand. You should keep your hand in this position for about forty-five seconds. By the end of that period, you'll have the information you've been trying to think of.

Of course, if you're left-handed perform this activity with the opposite hands.

Visualization and Association

Have you ever seen "memory performers" on television? These are individuals who entertain – and astound – you with their amazing recall of items, facts, and figures.

You're no doubt watched one of these individuals and lamented you wished you had a memory even half as good. The truth of the matter is that they have done nothing that you can't do yourself. They weren't born with that amazing memory, they just learned and perfected the technique called "visualization and as-sociation" and very often called visualization.

By learning this technique, you'll be able to greatly accelerate the speed at which you'll learn, The prem-ise of this method is that the human brain can recall images far better and quicker than any other form of learning.

Why? Because believe it or not, images are less ab-stract than a myriad of facts and figures. You can re-call an image of your childhood home, for example, long after you've forgotten the home telephone num-ber that went with it.

What you do in the visualization process is to convert your abstract information into an image. This image is called a mental hook, which means that once you re-call that, the other information you've associated with it will surface.

This is a great method of memory retrieval for those persons who have a difficult time focusing on their work. The very act of visualization forces your mind to focus and pay more attention to the material at hand.

Think back to the last time you were introduced to somebody new. Did you remember her name the first time it was mentioned to you? If you're like most of us, you probably didn't. And if you're like most of us you spent the rest of the conversation, hoping she would repeat it. Usually to no avail. Sometimes your only alternative was too embarrassed to ask her to repeat it.

The visualization method is much simpler to use than you may think at first glance. You may have already used it without knowing it. Here's a good example of the method that we all learned. If someone asked you to draw the shape of the country of Germany, you'd be hard-pressed to do (unless of course, it's your home country).

Now, if someone asked you to draw the shape of Italy, you'd be able to at least complete a rough outline of it, because we all know that the country is in a shape of a shoe. Similarly, many students learn the names of the five great lakes through visualization.

Even before you even think about the names of the lakes, create an image of five houses sitting in a row on a large lake. But don't think of these images as houses. Instead, call them homes. Now, you'll have no trouble recalling the names. Take the letters in the word homes and you have all five lakes: Huron, Ontario, Michigan, Erie, and Superior.

This technique can also help you remember certain items on your grocery list. Let's say you're going to the grocery store and among the items you intend to buy are blueberries. How would you go about doing this? What about creating an image of you atop a gigantic blue bear heading toward the store. Your mind will instantly convey that image into the need to purchase the blueberries.

If you use even a fraction of the memory-strengthening secrets in your next study session, you'll see that the learning process will be less painful and far more beneficial.

CHAPTER 6:

╰✤╯

Remove Potential Distractions

Before you even sit down to study or learn any piece of new information, the very first thing you should do is remove every potential distraction from your workspace. While it's a simple task it's not one most people like to do.

This means first and foremost you need to turn off your cell phone. At the very least place it in airplane mode. For the time you're studying, you'll survive. In this way, you'll not be bothered by phone calls, email notifications, and text messages.

But more than that, you won't be tempted to take "a five-minute" break to play a video game on your phone that extends into a half-hour or more.

1. You'll want to turn off the television.

You've probably seen that episode of The Big Bang Theory three times, so why are you putting aside your studies to get involved in it one more time. Even if your argument is that you need a background noise, you'll undoubtedly get pulled into whatever is on that TV.

2. Do whatever you need to stay away from the internet.

It's just one more way to check your email. It also contains dozens of sites that you can get lost in, from Facebook to Pinterest to Twitter. And whatever else the current popular social media venue is. You certainly can view these sites as a reward after you've met your studying goals. But don't look while you're trying to learn.

3. Don't multitask.

Oh, you'll be so tempted to do this. Some individuals appear to seamlessly study five different subjects or topics at one time. They flit from one topic to another to a third . . . well, you get the idea.

It's far more effective if you block off a good amount of time for one subject and then give it your full attention. Why? For one reason you give yourself time to actually become engaged in the topic – remember the immersion technique. It's difficult to experience immersion in fifteen minutes or less.

4. Forget about micro-focusing

What is micro-focusing? That's when you read the textbook or study the material word for word

Some students think the best studying is slow studying. Reading every word, one by one, writing every sentence of the paper, one by one, preparing one's presentation, one word at a time. But like any cognitive activity, studying is a process that takes place over time and gains strength by building up speed. If you focus too narrowly on the individual elements of what you're doing, you suck the life out of the learning process and disrupt the intellectual growth that's possible, even in studying.

5. Create a Study Routine

Life is nothing if not chaotic. Far too often "the chaos" whatever form it takes in your life, has the potential to get out of control and running over your well-intentioned priorities. In order to prevent this from occurring, an article in the Harvard Business Review urges you to adopt rituals in both your daily and weekly schedules.

Once you establish a ritual, then follow it . . . well, religiously. This will help your mind and your body maintain the necessary focus to learn quicker. Of course, as time goes by, these rituals will no doubt evolve to remain an effort force in your habits. You'll also want to remain flexible, if the ritual you initially have chosen isn't working, don't immediately blame it on yourself, try changing and adjusting your ritual. You'll eventually create a ritual that not only you can live with, but flourish by it.

6. Recite a mantra

Sometimes the distractions don't come from the external environment but from your own mind. Even if you've removed all electronic paraphernalia from your study area, ensured everyone was quiet and turned off everything else that had the potential to be distracting, you still may find that you're plagued with distractions. Your mind is reeling with all sorts of thoughts – and not one of them deals with any of the topics you're studying.

Don't give up. Instead, recite a mantra that reminds you to focus on your studies again. Some experts say that something as simple as "be here now." It's short, simple and to the point. But more than that, the mantra, in three words, reminds you to re-focus and live in the present.

You can learn whatever mantra you discover works best for you. The only goal of this short phrase it to steer your mind back to your purpose at work – accelerated learning.

7. Announce your Intentions

That's right! If you're not leaving the house to study, then make sure every other person in the house knows of your intentions. You don't have to make a big deal out of this period of studying. Make sure that individuals are aware you're studying and would like not to be distracted for the next couple of hours. If you've ever meditated, then you know how important it is to let others know what you're planning.

Believe it or not, when people know you're looking for some quiet time alone, they're more than happy to provide you with it.

Accelerated learning can change your life, there's no doubt about it. By removing distractions and keeping your mind on the task at hand, you'll discover how quickly "accelerated learning" can work in your life.

Conclusion

The legendary American educator and methodologist, Edgar Dale, created a hierarchy of the way in which the mind learns. While he did not assign the percentages, you see next to them, other educators and specialists in the learning field did.

Today they are statistics that are nearly on the mark regarding our degree of retaining what he learned. We retain:

10 percent of what we read

20 percent of what we hear

30 percent of what we see

50 percent of what we see and hear

70 percent of what we discuss with others

80 percent of what we personally experience

95 percent of what we teach others

In a very real sense, those statistics represent the heart and soul of this book. Accelerated learning, the ability to learn more material in a shortened time span, is not achieved through on method.

You can't learn anything by handling the material once, as Dale in his hierarchy of learning implies here. While it's true we each have a flair for learning more quickly using visual aids over words or hands-on experience. Those are certain characteristics we all have and need to use to our best advantage.

But it takes a wide array of methods, a myriad of techniques and a focus and determination to do so.

More than that, you can't confuse the concept of learning with the act of memorizing facts and figures. The latter method may be excellent if you want to remember something in the short term. It is of no use, however, if you really want it to become embedded in your brain and be able to recall it months or even years from now. That's where true learning plays a vital role. The knowledge you've truly learned stays with you for a long time – some of it forever.

So the more you know about how you learn, the better you can adjust your learning style to be the best possible receptacle for the new information headed your way.

Don't be misled. Just because you've finished reading this book, that doesn't mean your learning process is complete. Learning, as you probably are already well aware is a lifetime activity. Regardless of your age, scientists now know you can learn just about anything you've set your mind to. At one time, these same scientists were convinced your learning capacity diminished as you aged. In other words, there was only a short span of time in your life when you were at your peak with regard to learning.

After that peak age, you may still be able to learn, but not at the accelerated rate that many have mastered today. That's one of the beauties of learning faster. It, indeed, can be performed however old you are.

The exercises, methodologies, and techniques of learning provided in this book are only the tip of the iceberg in regard to your ability to digest the concept of accelerated learning.

There's more learning in your future. Guaranteed. And with the help of Pareto's Law – the Rule of 80-20 and many other tips for efficient, effective learning, you'll find yourself more confident than ever to meet the challenges – regardless of how quickly the information in the world increases.

BONUS CHAPTERS

Thinking Outside The Box

H ow to Think Creatively By Applying Critical Thinking and Lateral Thinking

Bruce Walker

INTRODUCTION

~

"Thinking outside the box".

It's a phrase that has been used for nearly forty years now. For many in the corporate world, it has become a cliché -- so much so, you've problem heard it in any number of commercials. That doesn't mean the idea behind it isn't a powerfully useful instrument for your daily life because it is.

Despite its overuse as a term, it's without a doubt one of the most potent methods you can improve the quality of your life, gain more time -- and even begin dipping your feet into the waters of your dream career.

You may assume that since out of the box thinking is such a cliché in the business world that it has no place in your personal life. Think again. Cliché or not it's still one of the most valuable and necessary assets many of us have -- even if we don't know it's bubbling just below the surface of our consciousness.

Consider the term "life hacks" which has caught on with people on the internet in the past few years. It's nothing more -- or should we say nothing less - than thinking out of the box. Have a space problem in your home that needs to be solved or you'll be sleeping on the front porch because you're out of room in your bedroom? Nothing less than out of the box thinking may help you keep your stash of precious items and allow you to sleep in your bed tonight.

Out of the box, thinking implies a marvelous twist of the mind. It levels the playing field between you and the likes of Albert Einstein, Steve Jobs, and Thomas A. Edison. We're not saying you're about to create the next great computer, the latest revolutionary theory of the universe or something that will replace the electric lightbulb. But you'll be able to turn your personal life on its head and begin to love life again.

What is Thinking Outside The Box?

In a nutshell, the phrase means to tackle a problem with creative or novel thinking, attacking the situation from an unusual or unexpected perspective. Take, for example, the cliché we've all heard: When life hands you lemons, make lemonade. That's out of the box or creative thinking. Taken one level higher, the thinker who kicks the box to the side of the road is the one who after making lemonade, launches his own multi-million-dollar lemonade business.

Some of the nation's most successful industrialists and entrepreneurs have been thinking creatively -- viewing problems from a perspective the other business people couldn't or wouldn't think of. Thomas Edison, who nearly single-handedly drove the Industrial Revolution in the early twentieth century once said: "It's hard to think about achieving the impossible when you're surrounded with people wanting to discuss only the possible."

He probably found more inventions and innovations on the road to creating something else than most inventors or industrialists. One idea inevitably led to another. He, in effect, refused to limit his thinking to the conventional way of doing

Then there's Albert Einstein. Most people don't consider scientists as being very creative. But if anyone could prove that stereotype wrong, it would be Einstein. Asked how he came up with the theory of relativity. He first imagined himself riding a beam of light, traveling at 186,000 miles per second. Have you ever thought of that?

You're sitting back in your chair right now, thinking, "But I'm no Thomas Edison and definitely no Einstein." That very well could be true, but have you ever really put yourself to the test? Have you ever tried to put creative thought into your daily life?

But for your purposes -- especially if you're not used to putting such creativity into your thinking -- your thought process doesn't need to be such a dramatic change of perspective. Something as simple as re-purposing an unused ladder into a unique-looking bookcase is a perfect example of thinking out of the box.

You can use this creative approach to any aspect of your life. Yes, you can. Don't think it takes any special education. Don't believe that you have to label yourself "creative" in any way to be able to think creatively.

Many individuals mistakenly believe that only writers, actors, and artists are creative. What they fail to consider is that all of us, in our ways, can be creative -- whether we recognize it at the moment or not.

There must be something that you'd like to view from a different perspective in your life -- from changing your economic position to learning a new set of life skills, to being more content with your surroundings. After all, if you're curious about the idea of "thinking outside of the box," then you're probably eager to give it a try.

How the Phrase Even Came to Be? (9 Dots Puzzle)

The origins of the phrase are fuzzy, but one thing is known. It comes from what's referred to as the "nine-dot" puzzle. Arrange nine dots on a piece of paper so there are three rows of three dots each. Now you can visualize what this puzzle looks like. Individuals were asked to connect the dots without lifting their pencil from the paper *and* ensuring that all nine dots are used.

Most individuals who try this, think that the lines they're drawing must stay within the confines the "box" the outer dots have created. But if you read the instructions again, that's not specified anywhere. Once you begin to think out of the confines of the box the dots created then you can find multiple solutions to the puzzle.

Go ahead and draw those nine dots right now and give it a try. What's impossible when you think one way suddenly becomes easy when you view it from a different perspective.

Are you an "out of the box" or a creative thinker? Below is a quick quiz to test your ability to do just that. You'll find the questions first. Following the questions, are the answers with a rough generalization of where your thinking aligns. The answers, as well as a rough evaluation of your current level of creative thought, are revealed below the quiz. (Don't get nervous! Approach this quiz as a game!)

How Creative Are You? Quiz

1. I have five apples and I take away three. How many apples do I have?

2. A plane crashes on the border of Germany and Poland. Where do you bury the survivors?

3. A bus explodes on the US-Canada border. Where do you bury the dead?

4. In what sport are the shoes made of metal?

Soccer

Horseracing

Badminton

Basketball

5. John's mother has four children. Three of them are named April, May, and June. What's the name of her fourth child?

6. Is it legal for a man to marry his widow's sister?

7. A man built a rectangular house with a southern view on all four sides. He looked out the window and saw a bear. What color was the bear?

8. If you were alone in a deserted house at night and there were an oil lamp, a candle, and firewood and you only have one match, which would you light first?

9. A farmer has 15 cows. All but 8 dies. How many cows does he have left?

10. You drove a bus leaving Canterbury with 35 passengers, dropped off 6 and picked up 2 at Eversham picked up 9 more at Sittingbourne, dropped off 3 at Chatham, and then drove on to arrive in London 40 minutes later, what color are the driver's eyes?

Answers:

1 3 apples

2. You don't bury survivors

3. In a cemetery

4. Horseracing

5. John

6. By definition, if the man has a widow, then the man is deceased.

7. The bear was white. It was a polar bear and the house was built at the North Pole.

8. The match

9. 8 cows

10 You're the driver.

Evaluate your Score

8 - 10 right. Congratulations! You're already a creative thinker. You can use this book to help boost your current seemingly natural ability.

6 - 7 You're not bad at this thinking out of the box. Once you start reading this book, you'll be able to develop this skill even further.

5 and below. You haven't been called upon to use your creative thinking. This book will help you do a better job of thinking outside the box.

How to Use this Book

This book is easy enough to use. Read through the entire book once, if you can, before you start putting any of the exercises or ideas into action. Of course, if you can't wait to put your new-found creativity into action, by all means, feel free to do so while the urge and desire are ignited.

What will you discover in this book to help you polish your innovation? You'll learn the essential exercises to spark your creative approach to problem-solving and how you can use this to your advantage. You'll be surprised at how many of the successful business people already know -- but seldom talk about -- thinking outside of the box.

Along those same lines, you'll discover exactly what lateral thinking is and how using this can help you find more creative solutions to your everyday problems -- the big ones and the smaller irritations.

You'll also learn that as much as creative or out of the box thinking is required on a daily basis, you can't put it into effect efficiently without using lateral and critical thinking processes alike. That's why there are chapters devoted to reminding you exactly what these are.

Are you ready to start a new life -- one of being free of "the boxed thinking" that may be holding you back? Then you need to start reading Chapter 1 right now.

CHAPTER 1:

~

The Invisible Trap of Social Standards

Mary sat with her friends at the cafe. They were talking about their daily routines. "Sometimes I just get tired, believe it or not, of doing the same thing day after day. Don't get me wrong. I love my family and I wouldn't change them for the world. But, sometimes, I just think I need some spice in my life." She paused a moment and added. And I don't mean an affair."

Is that how you feel about your life? Do you look back at your high school days and even college days and think back to how much more creatively you thought back then? If you wanted to pack your suitcase and head for a trip to New York City or San Francisco or just wander aimlessly for a weekend, you'd do it.

Today, if you tried that there would probably a chorus of a thousand voices telling you socially responsible people just don't do that. You must plan these things out. You have to make sure you get the right airline ticket price. And God forbid you to take your car. What would happen if it broke down?

Even if you haven't yearned to travel, you're probably like most of us, you approach it from just about every aspect of your life from "the box." Most of us are rather satisfied with this life. Many individuals refer to this as their comfort zone. It's the area or activity in which they feel at ease.

This is the zone in which we accept who we are in life and where we are. After all, wasn't this the purpose of growing up and becoming an adult, to fit into society with a minimum of disturbance? And having a "comfort zone" is much better than constantly feeling anxious, feeling as if something bad is about to happen, but not knowing when or even why.

Comfort Zone or Stagnation?

But there's also a danger in that comfort zone and it's called *stagnation*. With that content, for some, comes the inability to see life any differently than what it is right now.

There's a theory that you're the average of the five people you associate with. What that usually means is you've adopted the social standards of these people. You've either adopted their interests or sought these friends and kept them because of your shared interests, similar careers or any other number of reasons. Support groups, by the way, are built on this concept.

If your friends are video gamers, for example, you're far more likely to be one as well. If they're interested in crafting, the chances are good that you'll be interested in that hobby too.

And that is where the "box" comes in. As long as you're following the social standards of the group spend time with, you're probably not thinking outside of the box -- you may not even recognize that you're in a box. You certainly don't consider yourself "trapped." Or perhaps you do.

Either way, you're reading this book, which is probably an indication you're interested in jumping out of your box and getting out of your comfort zone. Why is it difficult for many of us to step out of our comfort zone, think outside of the box and think differently from the rest of the group?

When was the last time you stopped to think about what you really wanted -- and still want -- out of the life? Do you allow yourself to dream of an awesome vacation or start writing that blog? Do others shoot your thoughts down right away, telling you it's a waste of time? So you return to your comfort zone and working within your box.

You do know it doesn't have to be that way, don't you? You can defy social standards and begin to do the things you've always wanted to do, the way you wanted to do them.

So, what's stopping you -- besides those so-called friends? Sure, their intentions are sincere, but ultimately you have to do what you feel is best for you. If you're wary of playing video games with them, tired of facing another scrapbook party without moaning and groaning about it or even can't take another episode of some "true crime" television show, then it's time to examine what's holding you back.

Here are several reasons why most of us are fearful of looking at life from any perspective than the one we've always have, that is our box.

1. But we've always done it this way.

Have you ever seen this sentiment in a poster: "But, we've always done it this way." That is the biggest reason people resist change. In effect, they're saying that everything is perfectly fine the way it is. You'll hear this same sentiment expressed as "Why change horses in midstream?" This is their way of rationalizing their efforts to stay within their comfort zone.

You may have even heard the saying "If it ain't broke, why fix it?" These people are conveying the exact sentiment. The general opinion is that if something -- anything -- has served us well for so long, "don't rock the boat". When you do try to change things or "fix" things, you may be making things even worse.

2. Trapped by your own personal method of thinking.

You along with everyone else around you may be locked into a familiar, comfortable way of thinking. Up until this moment, you may never have even thought about doing anything differently. Why everyone around you is doing basically the same things and they seemed perfectly satisfied. Your dissatisfaction, you presume, only means there's something wrong with you -- not with the social norms.

Because of this, you approach your problems from a limited point of view. Of course, we have always done it this way -- who am I to even dream of doing it another way. You can blame your "inner critic" for censoring your potential "out of box thinking."

3. Trapped by your emotions.

Stepping into the realm of creativity -- especially if you haven't been thinking in that way for a while -- can be intimidating, to say the least. As you've already seen, you find yourself straying from your comfort zone. That leads you into an uncomfortable realm. It's here you're more than likely begin to feel a general anxiety growing. As you begin to think differently, you're entering an unknown world, filled with "what if" incidents. What if, one of those options you're considering is less than optimal?

Or worse yet, what if you take this momentous step and your friends and family think you weird? What, if after all is said and done, the outcome is embarrassing to you -- or even painful in some way?

What you may not realize that all of these emotions are just different ways your body resists change. It's hoping that you'll eventually cave into these fears and qualms and just plain procrastinate on this concept -- whatever it may be.

4. It's hard to be creative with personal problems hanging over your head.

If you're beating yourself up because you can't, for the life of you, think outside of the box, you may want to stop and examine your life for a moment. Are you going through some personal crisis or problem? It's hard to be creative when you're struggling with a major life change. You may be experiencing financial hardships at the moment or even going through an emotional event like a divorce. At these or similar points in your life, it's all most of us can do to just hold our own with the life we have.

Sometimes, though, this is the time when you may be digging up some of the oldest and deepest held regrets about what you *didn't* do with your life and you begin to daydream about "what might have been."

If this is the case, you still may want to wait to make any type of creative changes in your life. If you ignore these issues and continue to plow through with trying to be creative anyway, you may be just setting yourself up for failure.

5. Searching for the "right" answer

You've probably learned this habit in school. Every question, according to the tests you've taken in school, has either a right or wrong answer. Think about how many true and false tests you've taken and how many multiple-choice quizzes you've sat through. After approaching education in this fashion, you may discover your creativity stilted, at least initially, by considering whether what you're planning falls in one of these two categories either right or wrong.

Without a doubt, there are advantages to this categorization habit, but it does nothing to further your creative thinking. Right about now, you may be thinking that a three-week vacation to New York City is in order. But one of your dearest friends tells you this isn't the right time. That's not the proper decision right now.

Never mind the fact that this might be the "right" answer for you to clear your mind for a while. Or perhaps you've made a decision on some other aspect of your life, but here again, someone or your instincts tell that isn't the "right" answer for you.

It hinders you "out of the box" thinking. Once you realize that the vast majority of issues we deal with on a daily basis can't be viewed in either black or white. There is a spectrum of shades of gray that can lead you to happiness. Issues that pop up in real life usually have more than one answer. When someone tries to assign a right or wrong way to a problem or try to impose one on you, they're missing the valued concept that the issue may have more than one "right" answer.

6. Viewing creative, outside of the box thinking as "destructive."

Hear me out on this one. Perhaps you don't even realize you're thinking this, it may be so ingrained and enmeshed in your thinking. If you choose a different way of doing even something as simple as changing your morning routine, your subconscious may feel that it's being a destructive force in the world. After all, if someone wanted to point at you and accuse you of ripping the fabric of society as we know it apart, he might be right. "Rules," they may say "are that simple and are created for a reason. Who are you to deviate from them? What makes you special?"

You may believe, at first glance, that this is a block that makes little or no sense. But you'd be amazed at how many individuals follow all the rules, even though they aren't working for them. There's a person

I spoke to once who said before she takes any specific actions, she asks herself, "How does this serve me?" If it doesn't serve her -- make her life better in some way -- she tosses that "rule" aside. Step by step, she's remaking her life in a very creative way, by thinking out of your own box.

Have you noticed that that people praise and admire some of the most creative thinkers in the business world? Think about Richard Branson and his marvelous success and the brave moves he made to make it happen. But they refuse to break even a small rule in their life. Perhaps you should think twice before you start admiring someone like Branson -- and start breaking some rules of your own.

Seriously. Are you ready to consider not only thinking outside of the box but actually kicking it wide open and allowing some truly creative thoughts into your life? Then you're ready to move to the next chapter. That's where we'll get the process moving.

CHAPTER 2:

∼

Kicking the Box Open and Sparking your Creativity

Many people get excited about the idea of thinking outside of the box and kick it to the curb immediately only to discover that after years of conventional thinking, it's a bit more difficult than they had imagined. And that makes sense. After years of thinking one way, it's not easy to allow your mind to be "liberated" and allow it to run wild.

Before you attempt to jump into creative thinking, you may want to "exercise your brain." Don't worry, these aren't as tough as you may believe. It's hard to start thinking in a manner you're not accustomed to.

To be truthful, that's not your fault. So don't beat yourself up if the creative thoughts don't flow immediately. Your brain has been used to thinking in a certain manner and it will take some time for it to rewire itself and adjust to another thought process. It'll be slow going at first, but as you continue to do it, your brain catches on and works faster at it. Guaranteed.

Your brain is no different from any other muscle in your body. If you don't use it, then it slowly gets weaker. That's the bad news. The good news, though, is that it's easy enough to strengthen this muscle just as you would any other one in your body: through regular exercise.

At first, when your "creative thinking muscles" are initially called into action after perhaps years of unused, you may turn around and find yourself wandering aimlessly through your house, wondering where and how to begin this valuable thought process.

Many fiction writers find that every morning upon arising they need to get their "creative juices" flowing by writing three to five pages of . . . well, nothing. Their goal is to write anything that pops into their minds. Hopefully, some of these covers what their subconscious minds have unearthed while they slept. But if they can't recall what they dreamed of or any words that came mind then basically, they're instructed to write anything. It may be something as simple as "I need my morning coffee."

Once they clear their minds and got their neurons moving in full speed, they inched themselves out of their box and into their projects, whatever those may be. Believe it or not, it works more often than not....

Thank you for reading The Fast Learner's Guide. If you like and find this book helpful. Please take some time to share your thoughts and post a review. It'd be greatly appreciated.

I wish you the best and good luck!

Bruce Walker

www.ingramcontent.com/pod-product-compliance
Lightning Source LLC
Chambersburg PA
CBHW031132020426
42333CB00012B/339